# BARTIMAEUS

## ARE YOU LIKE BARTIMAEUS

## PASTOR RON

WESTBOW
PRESS®
A DIVISION OF THOMAS NELSON
& ZONDERVAN

WestBow Press books may be ordered through booksellers or by contacting:

WestBow Press
A Division of Thomas Nelson & Zondervan
1663 Liberty Drive
Bloomington, IN 47403
www.westbowpress.com
844-714-3454

ISBN: 978-1-6642-5725-2 (sc)
ISBN: 978-1-6642-5727-6 (hc)
ISBN: 978-1-6642-5726-9 (e)

Library of Congress Control Number: 2022902374

Print information available on the last page.

WestBow Press rev. date: 02/03/2022

# PREFACE

I was introduced to the figure of Bartimaeus by Dr. Walter Malone Jr., pastor of Canaan Christian Church in Louisville, Kentucky, in his book *An Operative Faith for Oppressed People.* When I was a member of Canaan, Dr. Malone opened up the scriptures to me through his teaching in a way that I had never seen before. I am forever grateful for Dr. Malone and his teaching.

Ever since I was introduced to Bartimaeus, I have been intrigued by him. It was there at Canaan that I realized God was calling me into the ministry. Now being in the ministry and pastoring, I have enjoyed studying Bartimaeus, and I account my study of the Word of God to a wonderful man of God, Dr. Charles Baker, my father in the ministry, who challenged me to be accurate in my preaching and teaching by studying and verifying what I preached and taught in God's word. Dr. Baker gave me so much by providing study material and advice purchasing books that assisted me in my studying and training.

I must also give praise to Dr. John Long, my Old Testament, New Testament, and Greek professor at Western Kentucky University. I sat under him and feasted on the knowledge he shared, and I drew from him as I spent hours of class time and personal time around him.

I thank God for these men who have shaped me and given me direction in my ministry and life. These men are the reason I have taken the time to look into the Gospel of Mark and discover things about Bartimaeus. I have prayerfully studied this text, and God has spoken into my life over the years as I pondered the many questions that have arisen from the attention I have given Bartimaeus. All scripture references are from the New King James Version Bible unless otherwise noted.

Most important, I thank my wife, Rev. Dr. Sharon Whitlock, who looks over my shoulder and challenges me to be structural in my writing. She ask me hard questions to verify the direction and content of my writing. Thank you so much, sweetheart. I appreciate your help and support.

I also thank our church family, New Beginnings Christian Ministries, for their support and prayers.

It is my desire that you will come away with many questions answered and a view of Bartimaeus that only God can give you. My prayer for each reader is that you see yourself in the person of Bartimaeus in your walk with Jesus and that you share your experiences with Bartimaeus and those around him with others as God gives you the opportunity. I pray that you are truly blessed by this work, and may God truly bless you.

Sincerely in love with Jesus,
Pastor Ron E. Whitlock Sr.

# INTRODUCTION

In the Gospel of Mark, we find a certain blind man named Bartimaeus. He is mentioned only once in scripture, and no other gospel writer identifies this man and his father but Mark. We find blind men that Jesus healed in all the gospels, but only here do we find a blind man named Bartimaeus. The Gospel of Mark, being the first of the four gospels written, focuses on how Jesus ministers to the physical and spiritual needs of others. If you have viewed the television show *Downton Abbey*, you have some sense of a servant's role and their position in life.

As I take note of Mark's gospel, I notice that Mark does not take the time to mention many people's names. This action-packed, fast-moving gospel might be compared to an action movie. Mark uses the word "and" more than a thousand times in this gospel, and Jesus is presented as moving quickly from one scene to the next in a chain of event after event linked by words such as *immediately, straightaway, behold*, and *departed*.

The Gospel of Matthew presents Jesus as the King, the teacher, and "lion-like." Every king has a lineage, and we find in the gospel of Matthew the lineage of Jesus from Abraham to Joseph, Jesus's earthly father. The Gospel of Luke presents Jesus as the perfect man, man-like, and every man has a birth record, as does the Son of Man, as Luke records Jesus's birth records back to Adam. The Gospel of John presents Jesus as the mighty God, eagle-like, but with God there is neither beginning nor end—He is from everlasting to everlasting. John 1:1–2 says, "In the beginning was the Word, and the Word was with God, and the Word was God. He was in the beginning with God" (NKJV).

But here in the Gospel of Mark, we are given a view of Jesus as a servant. He is presented as being ox-like, and Mark lists the miracles He performed. Jesus's birth is not mentioned, the shepherds are not present, and there is no visit from the wise men from the east. But Mark begins with John baptizing Jesus, and the ministry of Jesus begins. How fitting this is, because a lowly servant has no introduction nor do those whom he is serving want to know about him, his family lineage, or his past. They only want to be served by a servant. The Gospel of Mark highlights Jesus's work as a servant.

Matthew 20:29–34 speaks of two blind men being healed as Jesus comes out of Jericho. Luke 18:35–43 speaks of a blind man calling out to Jesus near Jericho, but because

Mark is the first gospel written and Matthew and Luke may have gotten their information from Mark's gospel, I have chosen to stay basically with Mark's version, which focuses on Jesus's role as a servant looking toward the cross, serving man and representing man even in His death. It would seem as if Mark's mission of writing was to show Jesus's life as a servant to man and His death for man on the cross. This is also illustrated in Mark 15:39: "So when the centurion, who stood opposite Him saw that He cried out like this and breathed His last, he said, 'Truly this Man was the Son of God!'" (NKJV).

In the midst of this action-packed drama, Mark mentions the man Bartimaeus. As I stated earlier, Mark does not take time to mention the names of many of the people Jesus encounters because of how fast this gospel moves. Jesus goes from one setting to another, one scene to another, one backdrop to another backdrop. This perked my interest, and questions arose in my mind. Who is this Bartimaeus? Why is he mentioned only here, and no one else mentions his name? Why is his father's name mentioned? We know he follows Jesus toward Jerusalem, but where does he go after this? Why did those around him try to stop him? And there are many other questions that I try to address in the following pages. Over the years more insight has been given to me about Bartimaeus which has allowed me to put these revelations together in this book. It is amazing how the Holy Spirit can give new reflections on the same scriptures and from a different angle. Also, some of this perceptiveness comes from spiritual growth and study.

I have concluded that in these few scriptures of the tenth chapter of Mark, we can find the complete role of the church and the members of the church and our work in society beyond the church walls.

# CHAPTER 1

## Only a Blind Man Saw Jesus

Now they came to Jericho. As He went out of Jericho with His disciples and a great multitude, blind Bartimaeus, the son of Timaeus, sat by the road begging. And when he heard that it was Jesus of Nazareth, he began to cry out and say "Jesus, Son of David, have mercy on me!"

Mark 10:46–47 NKJV

Jesus was on His way to Jerusalem for the last time in His earthly ministry. He traveled down the Jordan River valley, and going around Samaria entered into Judea and came into the city of Jericho. While on this journey, Jesus explained the importance of this trip to Jerusalem to the twelve:

Now they were on the road, going up to Jerusalem, and Jesus was going before them;

and they were amazed. And as they followed they were afraid. Then He took the twelve aside again and began to tell them the things that would happen to Him: "Behold, we are going up to Jerusalem, and the Son of Man will be betrayed to the chief priests and to the scribes; and they will condemn Him to death and deliver Him to the Gentiles; and they will mock Him, and scourge Him, and spit on Him, and kill Him. And the third day He will rise again. (Mk. 10:32–34 NKJV)

Yet James and John must have interpreted something totally different from what Jesus had said. Both of them wanted positions in an earthly kingdom they thought Jesus was to establish. These men had walked with Jesus, they were taught by Jesus, they had seen the miracles that Jesus had done, and they had been with the seventy disciples that were sent out by Jesus, yet they did not see Him as blind Bartimaeus saw Him. They only saw a man from God who would force the Roman oppressors out of their country, but Bartimaeus *saw* Jesus. Bartimaeus heard it was Jesus of Nazareth because the noise of the crowd got his attention.

Mark tells us of no other incidents that may have happened in Jericho, other than how they came to Jericho, and Jesus went out of Jericho with His disciples and a great multitude. This is important to note because of the way Mark's gospel is presented to us in portraying Jesus as a servant. Mark begins his gospel with Jesus being a man. There is no mention of His birth or childhood; Mark begins with His baptism then moves to His preaching. This gospel is action-packed, showing Jesus always on the move. Mark uses the word "and" over a thousand times, always showing Jesus in a series of actions, yet he never mentions anything happening in Jericho.

The question for us is, "What is Jesus doing in your city that the body of Christ is unaware of?" Is Jesus walking through your neighborhood, your city, but no one sees Him? What work in your city needs to be done that the church is unaware of? Are those who are blind to the church seeking to see Jesus, but our noise does not get their attention as the noise of Jesus traveling through Jericho got Bartimaeus's attention? Until we as the body of Christ quit trying to straighten out the pictures on the wall while not noticing the building is on fire, we will not help people see Jesus. Scripture tells us in Romans 10:14, "How then shall they call on Him in whom they have not believed? And how shall they believe in Him of whom they have not heard? And how shall they hear without a preacher?" We must get outside the church walls and allow people to see Jesus in us as we leave the protection of our Jericho, our sanctuary, our homes and neighborhoods, and serve others. Our challenge is to help people who are blind to the fact that Jesus is Lord to see Jesus in us and the work we do for Jesus.

A story is told of a statue of Jesus in a German town during World War II that His hands had been blown off during the bombing of that town. Someone put a sign on the statue that read "Jesus has no hands but yours." We are the hands and feet of Jesus. Dr. Tony Evans says, "We are the continuation of the incarnation." We must continue the work of Jesus. I define the church as "a body of baptized believers of Jesus Christ, called out and called into the service of Christ to continue the work of Jesus." It has been important to me to continue the work of Jesus, which is outside of our Jericho, our church walls. I pose these questions to you: are the blind (those who are blind to Christ) seeing Jesus in you? In your church, in your ministry, in your family, in the mirror? Are people seeing Jesus? Begin today to change what people see in you, and come away seeing Jesus even if no one else around you saw Him.

Bartimaeus was blind, but he could hear, and it was his hearing that enabled his seeing. Bartimaeus saw Jesus while he was still blind. Let me say that again: Bartimaeus sees Jesus while still blind. We must have a faith that works when we do not see through any situation we are in. We have been empowered by a spiritual vision that allows us to see Jesus in the midst of the storms of life. Your faith must be developed to a point that even if no one else sees Jesus, you must act on faith. *Faith is taking a blind step when you can't see where you are stepping.* Bartimaeus was willing to take a step of faith because He saw something that no one else could see, and that was Jesus changing his condition. He saw in Jesus the capability of being more than he ever had been in his life.

Bartimaeus saw in Jesus the potential he was pregnant with. It is only when we see Jesus that we see in Him the power to bring out of ourselves those gifts and talents we were born with. God designed you for a purpose, and Jesus empowers you to fulfill it, but you must see Him just as Bartimaeus "saw" Him. No matter how dark our vision gets, we must see Jesus when all others don't have a clue that Jesus is near.

Only a blind man saw Jesus. Bartimaeus was blind, but he had vision: "Where there is no vision, the people perish: but he that keepeth the law, happy is he" (Proverbs 29:18 KJV). The Hebrew word for "vision" in this verse is the Hebrew word, a verb *chazown* (pronounced "khaw-zone"), which involves gazing at, mentally perceiving, having a dream or a revelation. It should be obvious to us that the vision in this scripture is not about merely you just seeing with your eyes but is a prophetical seeing into your destiny.

Bartimaeus had a vision of himself seeing because he saw in Jesus the ability to change his situation. You must believe that God has created you for a divine purpose. It does not matter what you have gone through up till now or what you will face tomorrow, if you believe that your life is divinely purposed. You may not be living in your purpose right now, but do not judge your future on your present situation. Jesus can change your situation in a moment.

Mark does not mention that anyone else interacted with Jesus as He came out of the city of Jericho. Never let your blindness, the inability to see through your difficulties, stop you from calling out to Jesus. All hope is never gone. Have a vision for yourself always, even when others around you think you are ridiculous for your belief in Jesus as your answer. You must see Jesus at work in your life when no other person does.

# CHAPTER 2

## The Work of the Church

Now they came to Jericho. As He went out of Jericho with His disciples and a great multitude, blind Bartimaeus, the son of Timaeus, sat by the road begging. And when he heard that it was Jesus of Nazareth, he began to cry out and say, "Jesus, Son of David, have mercy on me!" Then many warned him to be quiet; but he cried out all the more, "Son of David, have mercy on me!" So Jesus stood still and commanded him to be called. Then they called the blind man, saying to him, "Be of good cheer. Rise, He is calling you." And throwing aside his garment, he rose and came to Jesus. So Jesus answered and said to him, "What do you want Me to do for you?" The blind man said to Him, "Rabboni, that I may receive my sight." Then Jesus said to him,

"Go your way; your faith has made you well."
And immediately he received his sight and
followed Jesus on the road.

Mark 10:46–52 NKJV

When I look at the ministry of the church, it reminds me of
this story about blind Bartimaeus, the son of Timaeus. In
fact, the body of Christ can be identified in this text. Each
of us can see ourselves in this text if we would look. Here are
six points to ponder in this passage.

First, Jesus is on the way to Jerusalem. Jerusalem represents
the place of God, the presence of God. The church should
always represent God and His presence, and the church
should point to God, just as Jerusalem was the place of God
in the temple. I'm reminded of a little boy who got lost.
Someone found him and called the police. The police asked
him his name. All the little boy could say was that his name
was Boo. They asked him his mother's name, and he said
"Mommy." So they drove him around the neighborhood,
and when the little boy saw the steeple of the church he
attended, he was able to point to his house down the street.
The church must always point us home, and our home is
being with God through our personal relationship with Jesus
and the presence of God that should reside in our churches.

Second, Jesus and His disciples are passing through

Jericho. We, the body of Christ, are sojourners passing through this pilgrim land. Too many Christians get bogged down with the things of this world and lose sight of heaven. I am not saying that you should not have anything; just don't let things have you. God wants you to be a good steward of all He places in your hands. Just know heaven is your home. You are to bringing the Kingdom of God everywhere you go.

Third, there is a great multitude of people traveling with Jesus and His disciples. There are multitudes of people just along for the ride who are not disciples and never intend to be disciples—they just want to be seen and to feel important. It is our work as the body of Christ, the church, to win people and get them to see Jesus as Savior and Lord.

Fourth, there are people on the sidelines of life who believe Jesus has passed them by. They are oppressed, depressed, suppressed, dispossessed, and sometimes even possessed. For the body of Christ, the Church, there are people on the sidelines of life and they feel as if no one cares about them and their situation. Their tears need to be wiped, and their stomach needs to be filled. Their hopes and dreams have been shattered, and they are sitting on the sidelines of life, needing a change in their lives without knowing how to go about getting it. They look at the church and don't want any part of that religion if the local or neighborhood church is not doing anything or not making a difference in people's lives. This is the continuing challenge for the church.

Fifth, Bartimaeus is the son of Timaeus and is blind. We are not told anything about his father, yet his father must have been known. The church must realize that people are the products of generations. What the parents are is sometimes what the children will be. They are blind to the possibilities of change and the Great Change Agent, the Holy Spirit. People are blind to the transforming power of Jesus. People are blind to who they are in Christ Jesus, and they never walk by faith into the great possibilities that life presents to us all.

Sixth, there are those who told Bartimaeus to be quiet and sit down. The church must realize that there are people who do not like others doing better than they are. Some are miserable, and they want you to be the same. They will do all they can to keep you down, and at the same time they do not realize that when they are keeping someone else down, they are keeping themselves down too.

Jesus is calling all of us out of our comfort zone and challenging us to move forward in Him and to continue the work that He started in the world. Now it is our move. Jesus has commissioned us in Matthew 28:19 (KJV) to "go ye therefore." We must represent Jesus in this world. He has chosen you for this work.

# CHAPTER 3

## What's in a Name?

Now they came to Jericho. As He went out
of Jericho with His disciples and a great
multitude, blind Bartimaeus, the son of
Timaeus, sat by the road begging.

Mark 10:46 NKJV

When you read the Bible, especially the Old Testament, you
will find that most of the names of the people mentioned
carry a meaning. For example, *Moses* means "to draw out
of water or to rescue out of water." *Abraham* means "father
of many nations", *Isaac* means "laughter," *Jacob* means
"supplanter," and *Jesus* means "Jehovah saves." So, as we
look at the name Bartimaeus, we want to know what his
name means as to each of us, our own name is the most
important name there is. This is a very true statement and I
have experienced it several times when important people in

high positions or well-known individuals remember and say my name. It just makes you feel good. On the other hand, if you don't name yourself, your circumstances and lot in life or the world will name you.

In this text, a blind man sits on the side of the road, begging as people go by. We know this man as Bartimaeus, the son of Timaeus. This is the only time his name appears in scripture. We find no other information about this man or his father. They seem to vanish from the pages of the New Testament. But as we look closer at the son of Timaeus, we find that we never know his real name—we know him as Bartimaeus, which in the Greek is γιος του Τίμαιος.

I have always made it a habit to call people I meet by their name. If someone is introduced to me with a nickname, I ask them what their real name is, and I call them by what they prefer. Most people will appreciate this, and it usually causes them to be more attentive when they are addressed by the name they prefer. There is just something special about being called by your name.

In our text, Jesus is on His way to Jerusalem, and as He passes through Jericho with His disciples and a great multitude of people, He encounters a blind man called Bartimaeus. But before Mark mentions his name, Mark tells us about his condition: he is blind (verse 46). This man called Bartimaeus is aware that something is going on and that a large crowd is approaching. He finds out that it is Jesus of Nazareth passing by, and he began to yell loudly, "Jesus Son of David, have mercy on me!" (Mk. 10:47 NKJV). He is told to be quiet, but he cries out the more to Jesus until Jesus stands still. Then Jesus tells someone to call the blind man. Jesus has not been told this man's name, nor was there any introduction. I have found out in life that it is never what others call you or what they do not call you; it is only important that Jesus calls you to Himself, just as Bartimaeus was called to come to Jesus. When Jesus calls us, we must respond to His call, just as Bartimaeus responded, and came to Jesus.

It is this man's condition that causes him to call out to Jesus. He had been identified by his condition, "blind," and probably everyone knew him as blind Bartimaeus. Too often, people are called by their condition. We see it many times in the Bible: the woman with the issue of blood (Mk. 5:25), a man who was a leper (Mk. 1:40), the paralytic man (Mk. 2:3), the young girl who had an unclean spirit (Mk. 7:25), and so many more, all identified by their condition. We are never told their names. But here we are told both Bartimaeus's name and his condition.

Often we meet people who are identified by their nickname, or their nickname identifies something about them. Willie, Jimmy, Shirley, Freddie, and Donna were all known by their nicknames. You know, I never understood why a big guy's nickname might be Tiny. So many people are identified by something other than their real name.

Sometimes certain families are known and identified by their last name. When we had a jail ministry, the jailers told my wife and I that they know the names of certain families who stay in jail all the time. During our jail ministry, we found it was not unusual to see a grandfather, father, and grandson in jail at the same time. Some people are connected by their physical, social, or other conditions by their name.

I remember the story of a young boy on his first day at school. This was way back in the day when we had neighborhood schools. The teacher was calling the roll, and everyone raised their hand except this boy. There were three names left, two children were absent, and only one child remained unnamed. So the teacher read the names that had not been responded to again, but the boy never raised his hand. The teacher asked the little boy his name. The boy gave his nickname. At that point, the teacher sent the little boy home to find out his real name. All his life he had been called by his nickname, and he did not even know his real name. That day was when he learned his real name. But although he learned his real name, he had difficulty responding to it.

It does not matter what others call you, but it does matter what you respond to when you are called. What is in a name? You must begin to look deep inside yourself and let Jesus bring out all the talents and gifts lying dormant, bursting to get out and become what God intended you to become.

There was something deep inside Bartimaeus, and that was a plan to get out of his condition if he ever met Jesus. Jesus never called Bartimaeus by his name. He just asked him, "What do you want Me to do for you?" (Mk. 10:51 NKJV). Jesus calls us out of our condition and brings new life, new hope, and new joy into our lives. We must respond to His call no matter what our name is or how we are identified.

What is in a name? I raise this question because as I looked at the name Bar-Timaeus, I found that the word *bar* means "son," meaning "the son of Timaeus." We find *bar* used in Matthew 16:17 when Jesus identifies Peter as being the son of Jonah. Mark identifies this blind man only as Timaeus's son. It would seem as if Timaeus is known to Mark's readers, the Romans for whom we understand he wrote this gospel to. We can understand that Bartimaeus is Jewish because he addresses Jesus as "the Son of David." And we understand from the Jewish Virtual Library, how the Jewish custom was and how they responded to alms-giving to those who were in need. So we can believe or accept that Bartimaeus was Jewish, but what is his name?

The name Timaeus, in Greek *Timaios*, as found in Strong's Exhaustive Concordance of the Bible, *Timaios* may also refer to a Chaldee word found in Hebrew as *taw-may*, which means "foul" in a religious sense of one who has made himself unclean or defiled. This information is found in *The complete Word Study Dictionary New Testament* using *Strong's Dictionary Lexical Aids Greek Concordance Translational Reference Index*. We understand that an unclean person could not go to the temple nor be around anyone who was considered clean. The Jews were very strict about this. Bartimaeus's condition of blindness meant he could not go into the temple because condition was considered unclean. His name did not matter; it was his condition that kept him away from the house of God.

There are many people who want to come to church and hear God's word preached, but their condition keeps them away. What others say about them, or maybe the way they think about themselves, keeps them away from the house of God. We must all remember where we were in life when Jesus found us. He found us in an unlovable state. Is it like Jesus to find us in an unlovable state and transform us into the family of God? It never matters what condition we are found in by Jesus; what matters is that He finds us and transforms us into the children of light.

What is in a name when a person needs to be found by Jesus? It does not matter what your name is—just call on *the* Name. Just say as Bartimaeus said, "Son of David have mercy on me!" (Mk.10:47). When Jesus responds to our request, we get an identity change, and our name is changed to a child of God. Just as Jesus changed Peter's name from Simon to

Cephas, Jesus changes Willie's name to a person willing to do His will. Jimmy is jumping for joy, Shirley is sounding sweet, Freddie is fasting and praying, and Donna is dancing because of joy in the Lord. Even Tiny is transformed and giving all praise to God. I know what Jesus can do for your life. He can change your name and your actions.

When Jesus changes our lives, people who knew the old you cannot recognize the new you. A singer by the name of Helen Baylor sings a song called "Look a Little Closer," in which she runs into an old friend who recognizes her but does not recognize the change that God has made in her life, so she tells the old friend to look a little closer. It does not matter what you were called in the past, Jesus gives us a new name and He calls us into our destiny. Bartimaeus was changed when he met Jesus.

What is so interesting about the Greek name Timaeus, which is spelled in Greek as *tau iota mu alpha iota omicron sigma*, is that if we change the ending from *iota omicron sigma* to just *omega*, the word is changed to *timao*, the verb *timo*, meaning "to honor, to have value or be valuable, or to revere." How fitting is the change in this word to the change Jesus made in Bartimaeus's life! We cannot return to the old way: just look at what Bartimaeus did after he received his sight—he followed Jesus in the way.

What is in a name? A name becomes more meaningful when Jesus authenticates us and directs our paths in our new life. Paul says in Philippians 3:13–14 (NKJV), "Forgetting those things which are behind and reaching forward to those things which are ahead, I press toward the goal for the prize of the upward call of God in Christ Jesus." We must move forward when Jesus changes our lives, especially if we have failed in an area of our lives. First John 1:9 (NKJV) says, "If we confess our sins, He is faithful and just to forgive us our sins and to cleanse us from all unrighteousness." We must move forward and follow Jesus in His way.

I noticed that Mark does not say that anyone in Jericho but Bartimaeus followed Jesus. Bartimaeus left those who wanted to keep him quiet and in his place. When Jesus comes into your life, there are people you need to get away from so that you can let God bring new people into your life. Remember your name has been changed now. What is in a name? A new *you* is within your name.

# CHAPTER 4

## Attitude

Now they came to Jericho. As He went out of Jericho with His disciples and a great multitude, blind Bartimaeus, the son of Timaeus, sat by the road begging. And when he heard that it was Jesus of Nazareth, he began to cry out and say, "Jesus, Son of David, have mercy on me!" Then many warned him to be quiet; but he cried out all the more, "Son of David, have mercy on me!" **So Jesus stood still and commanded him to be called. Then they called the blind man, saying to him, "Be of good cheer. Rise, He is calling you."** And throwing aside his garment, he rose and came to Jesus. So Jesus answered and said to him, "What do you want Me to do for you?" The blind man said to Him, "Rabboni, that I may receive my sight." Then Jesus said to him, "Go your way; your faith has made you well." And immediately he received his sight and followed Jesus on the road.

Mark 10:46–52 NKJV *(emphasis mine)*

Everything can be taken from a man but one thing: his attitude. To choose one's attitude in any given set of circumstances is to choose one's way. "Attitude" can be defined as the way you mentally look at the world around you. It is how you view your environment and your future. It is the focus you develop toward life itself. How do you view life? Is it "woe is me"? Or is it more like "I was born on the wrong side of the tracks, so now it is time to get on track with Jesus"?

In our text, we do not know how Bartimaeus, a blind man, became blind, but he had the right attitude. Nowhere do we see him complaining about his condition, nor do we see him blaming someone else for where he finds himself in life. Regardless of his circumstances, he expects to collect money from those who are passing by on their way to Jerusalem. His attitude has him standing on a busy road, not on a back road where few people travel. He could have chosen either road. He could have chosen a "woe is me" attitude, but instead he is expecting something because of where he has placed himself or according to the custom where others brought him. We can look at the man in Acts 3:2 who sat at the temple gate called Beautiful and was carried there daily. There are always people available to keep you in your situation. But it's your attitude that sets you up.

Let's look at the attitude of an NFL football player, Joe Theismann, who enjoyed an illustrious twelve-year career as quarterback of the Washington Redskins. He led the team in two Super Bowl appearances, winning in 1983 and losing the following year. He was entrenched in the record books as Washington's all-time leading passer. Still, the tail end of Theismann's career taught him a bitter lesson: Theismann says:

> I got stagnant. I thought the team revolved around me. I should have known it was time to go when I didn't care whether a pass hit Art Monk in the 8 or the 1 on his uniform. When we went back to the Super Bowl, my approach had changed. I was griping about the weather, my shoes, practice times, everything. Today I wear my two rings—the winner's ring from Super Bowl 17 and the loser's ring from Super Bowl 18. The difference in those two rings lies in applying oneself and not accepting anything but the best. *Source: Reader's Digest, January, 1982*

Theismann had an *attitude* problem in Super Bowl 18.

Bartimaeus's attitude gave him insight and helped him to deal with his disability, which was being blind. Your attitude can control your vision. Yes, even though Bartimaeus is blind, his attitude gave him vision. Consider the vision of the hummingbird and that of the vulture:

> Both the hummingbird and the vulture fly over our nation's deserts. All the vultures see is rotting meat because that is what they look for. They thrive on that diet. But hummingbirds ignore the smelly flesh of dead animals. Instead, they look for the colorful blossoms of desert plants. The vultures live on what was. They live on the past. They fill themselves with what is dead and gone. But hummingbirds live on what is. They seek new life. They fill themselves with freshness and life. Each bird finds what it is looking for. Source: Dr. James A. Scudder, "Hummingbird or vulture".

We all do. We find what we are looking for.

Bartimaeus's attitude was turned toward this new day. He could not change the past, nor did he waste time blaming someone for his condition. Most important, he was not allowing others with a bad attitude keep him from reaching toward his future. "Then many warned him to be quiet; but he cried out all the more, 'Son of David, have mercy on me!'" (Mk. 10:48 NKJV). There are two sides to the human personality, sides which pull us this way and the other, depending on our situation, our energy, and our commitment to being positive or negative. We have a choice of which side of the path we want to walk along—the one path is partly shady, and the other is partly sunny—or which cup to drink from—the one that's half empty or the one that's half full. It's the same path, and the same cup. We choose the attitude with which we view our world. The remarkable thing is we have a choice every day regarding the attitude we will embrace for that day. We cannot change our past. We cannot change the fact that people will act in a certain way. We cannot change the inevitable, the unavoidable. The only thing we can do is play on the one string we have, and that is our attitude. I am convinced that life is 10 percent what happens to me, and 90 percent how I react to it. And so it is with you: we are all in charge of our attitudes. It is all in the way you decide to view your situation.

When you're positive, you're anticipating successful encounters and people want to be with you. When you're negative, you're expecting the worst, and that is transmitted to those around you. That's when they start trying to avoid you. We all like people with positive attitudes.

Look at Bartimaeus. He would not quit. He would not

turn back. He would not give in. He would not throw in the towel. He would not slow down. He pressed on. If you want to be a winner in this race of Christianity, you must have a spirit of determination. Sometimes you have to put some energy and effort in what you are doing for the Lord Jesus Christ. Victory doesn't come easy. It takes a little sweat—no, let me rephrase that: it takes *a lot* of sweat.

Bartimaeus was asked by Jesus in verse 51, "What do you want Me to do for you?" In order to have a winning attitude, you must have discipline. First Corinthians 9:24–27 (NKJV) says:

> Do you not know that those who run in a race all run, but one receives the prize? Run in such a way that you may obtain it. And everyone who competes for the prize is temperate in all things. Now they do it to obtain a perishable crown, but we for an imperishable crown. Therefore I run thus: not with uncertainty. Thus, I fight: not as one who beats the air. But I discipline my body and bring it into subjection, lest, when I have preached to others, I myself should become disqualified.

We tend to think others have it better than we do. Everybody is either in a storm, just came out of a storm, or is headed into a storm. Matthew 5:45 (NKJV) says "that you may be sons of your Father in heaven; for He makes His sun rise on the evil and on the good, and sends rain on the just and on the unjust." Bartimaeus did not worry about the others around him. His attitude was set.

Here are three things Bartimaeus shows up about having a positive attitude.

1. Refuse to worry about those negative elements in your life that you can do nothing about. Bartimaeus not only heard it was Jesus of Nazareth with both ears, he used his ears to let the negative go in one ear and out the other ear.

2. When anticipating what lies ahead in a day, think about the good things that can happen. In verse 47, Bartimaeus cries out i "Son of David have mercy on me" over and over again.

3. We must know our purpose in life. No matter what happens in your life, purpose will always give you direction. Bartimaeus's purpose allowed him to respond to Jesus's question, "What do you want Me to do for you?"

God is faithful in always being with us in our trouble regardless of who causes it, even when we caused it:

Let your conduct be without covetousness; be content with such things as you have. For He Himself has said, "I will never leave you nor forsake you." So we may boldly say: "The Lord is my helper; I will not fear. What can man do to me?" (Heb. 13:5–6 NKJV)

As John Wooden said, "Things turn out best for people who make the best of the way things turn out." It isn't that some people have it better than others. We all have our trials and tribulations.

What attitudes do we cultivate? What are we thankful for this morning? What can I do for myself today? How can I help make my life better? How can I use my ability to bring joy into someone else's life? With the right attitude, you can know not to judge your future on your present situation. I don't know about you, but I realize whatever is over my head is underneath God's feet. And when I don't know what tomorrow holds for me, I remember who holds tomorrow. When it looks like I cannot get up, I look up, because if a man can look up, he can get up. There may be mountains in your way, but Jesus is a mountain mover. Jesus says in Matthew 21:21 (KJV), "Be thou removed and cast into the depths of the sea."

You may be going through something right now, but just hold on to God's unchanging hand. If you hold up, Jesus will show up and show the way out when He gets there. He may walk on water, or he may spit on the ground and rub it on your eyes for you to see your way through. He may feed five thousand and have some leftovers, or He just may speak to the winds and waves raging in your life. All I know is that Jesus will see you through. He will wipe tears from your eyes, and He always makes you see better than you saw before. He will turn your darkness into day. Weeping may endure for a night, but joy comes in the morning. Jesus is here, so it is morning time. Develop the right attitude. Bartimaeus had the right ATTITUDE.

# CHAPTER 5

## A Man with a Vision

Now they came to Jericho. As He went out of Jericho with His disciples and a great multitude, blind Bartimaeus, the son of Timaeus, sat by the road begging. And when he heard that it was Jesus of Nazareth, he began to cry out and say, "Jesus, Son of David, have mercy on me!" Then many warned him to be quiet; but he cried out all the more, "Son of David, have mercy on me!" So Jesus stood still and commanded him to be called. Then they called the blind man, saying to him, "Be of good cheer. Rise, He is calling you." And throwing aside his garment, he rose and came to Jesus. So Jesus answered and said to him, "What do you want Me to do for you?" The blind man said to Him, "Rabboni, that I may receive my sight." Then Jesus said to him,

"Go your way; your faith has made you well."
And immediately he received his sight and
followed Jesus on the road.

Mark 10:46–52 NKJV

The English writer John Heywood wrote, "There is none as blind as those who refuse to see." In our text, Jesus, the Savior of the World, is on His way to Passover for the last time. As was the custom, he traveled around Samaria then crossed back over the Jordan at Jericho. As He was coming out of Jericho, there on the side of the road was a blind man named Bartimaeus begging. This man is intelligent enough to be on the main road and to use all his senses, because he heard the noise of a great crowd of people coming, and he asked what was going on. The scripture tells us "when he heard that it was Jesus of Nazareth," he responded by yelling out "Jesus Son of David, have mercy on me!" Bartimaeus was a man with a vision. Isn't it something that in this text, it seems as if no one saw Jesus but a blind man? Mark records no one but Bartimaeus interacting with Jesus.

As I look at Bartimaeus being in a position to answer the question that Jesus asked him, I see four points I would like you to reflect on here.

**1. You must have a vision before an opportunity arises.** Too many people never realize an opportunity when it is presented because they do not have a vision. Bartimaeus did not wait until Jesus was gone over the hill and then wish he had called Him; he knew it was time to fulfill his plan. It did not matter how many people told Bartimaeus to be quiet and stay in his place. When you have a vision, it does not matter what the obstacles are. You fight to overcome all life's challenges when you have a vision driven by purpose.

**2. Having a vision will help you overcome any real or imaginary handicap that may or may not exist in your life.** Bartimaeus was blind but not as blind as those around him. He could not see Jesus, but with all his other senses he knew there was something different going on with the crowd that was passing by. You may be weak in one area, but God has blessed you in another area of your life. Work the gifts and talents that God has given you; use what you have to your advantage in furthering the Kingdom of God. God asked Moses, "What is that in your hand?" (Exodus 4:2 NKJV). Moses was able to take the rod and stretch it across the Red Sea. Moses was telling God how badly he stuttered. But God can use your stuttering. There was a man who stuttered but who ended up selling more Bibles than anyone in his church. He had a selling system he would use when he faced a reluctant buyer. He would stutter while asking people to buy a Bible but would offer to read it to them for free. This man had a plan and was ready for anyone who answered the door. They did not want to hear him stuttering through the whole Bible, so they purchased a copy, and on he went to the next house. Bartimaeus had a plan. He had a plan to get his sight. He had a vision that he could see in his own mind. It did not matter what other people thought of his plan—he just knew 'If I ever run across this Jesus, I have a plan."

**3. Having a vision will help you to overcome people who want to control or stop your progress.** If you do not have a vision and a plan for realizing your vision, you will never answer the question that Jesus proposes to you. What is it that *you* want Jesus to do for you? Bartimaeus answered, "Rabbi, that I may receive my sight." He did not ask for more people to pass by so he could collect more money, nor did he ask for a bigger house with a four-camel garage overlooking the Mediterranean Sea and facing a par-5 ninth hole on a golf course. Bartimaeus asked for something that would not return him to his yesterdays of having no sight. He had a vision of himself seeing. He knew it is the Messiah that turns dark yesterdays into bright tomorrows. This is the message for anyone who meets Jesus. Your life will never be the same. He stands still before us with His arms wide open, beckoning us to come. All Jesus, the blessed Messiah, wants is for us to follow Him in His purpose, His will toward your goal. But remember verse 48: "Then many warned him to be quiet; but he cried out all the more, 'Son of David, have mercy on me!'" Some things are systemic. One of the things we do in our ministry is to tell people, after getting to know their situation and capabilities, that we can get them off welfare and on to a better life. But there are so many people who do not want this welfare system to stop. They are like the people who told Bartimaeus to be quiet. We can wonder if people benefited from carrying him to this location each day? What would be their cut of his take of the day? How much money were they stealing from the blind man? Bartimaeus responded to Jesus's call. Those who had been holding him back now had to help him up so he could get to Jesus. They did not know what Jesus would do for him, nor did they know what Bartimaeus would ask for. They said to him "Rise, He is calling you."

**4. When we move toward Jesus, he is there with open arms to accept us, help us, and move us toward our vision.** Can you imagine being asked by Jesus "What do you want me to do for you?" *Do* you have a vision for your life? I challenge you to live life with a purpose and on purpose, and do not judge your future on your present situation. You need to know that sometimes it looks like you are down and out, but you must have a vision. Sometimes it looks as if you do not know which way to go, but you must have a vision. Sometimes it looks as if you are in the wrong and going the wrong way, but you must have a vision. Every now and then, it may seem that you have lost your way, but you must have a vision. Sometimes I cannot explain my situation, but I have a vision. Do you have a vision today? If you don't, just look toward Jesus. He will see you through. Whatever is over your head is under God's feet. Just keep on walking toward your vision. I am a witness that God will see you through—yes, He will. He will lift up a bowed down head, and wipe tears from your eyes. He will give hope to the hopeless

And finally, do not walk by rules of those who are on the sidelines of life. You have Jesus in you, and you can make a difference. The question is now, "Jesus, what do you want me to do for you?"

# CHAPTER 6

## A Thirsty Man and a Blind Woman

Now they came to Jericho. As He went out of Jericho with His disciples and a great multitude, blind Bartimaeus, the son of Timaeus, sat by the road begging. And when he heard that it was Jesus of Nazareth, he began to cry out and say, "Jesus, Son of David, have mercy on me!"

Mark 10:46–47 NKJV

A woman of Samaria came to draw water. Jesus said to her, "Give Me a drink." For His disciples had gone away into the city to buy food. Then the woman of Samaria said to Him, "How is it that You, being a Jew, ask a drink from me, a Samaritan woman?" For Jews have no dealings with Samaritans ... The

woman said to Him, "Sir, I perceive that You
are a prophet."

John 4:7–9, 19 NKJV

I have been pastoring church long enough to notice different
types of Christians in the church. Two types of people that
I will point out now are those who are thirsty and those
who are blind. One motivates, and the other stagnates. One
causes you to seek with a purpose, and the other causes you
to wander aimlessly. It is up to you to figure out which one
you are. The dictionary says that blindness is the inability to
see, and thirst is having a dry uncomfortable feeling in the
mouth or throat caused by having had nothing to drink. I
know someone reading this is saying, "He has got it wrong
in these scriptures—it is a blind man and a thirsty woman,"
so I say to you, just hang on and the Holy Spirit will show
you who is blind and who is thirsty.

Now as we look at Bartimaeus, the son of Timaeus, isn't
it wonderful that no matter what our condition is, Jesus
considers us highly prized? No matter how many times you
and I have blown it, no matter how many times we have
fallen, no matter how many times you said you were not
going to do something bad again but did anyway, if you truly
repent and run to the blood of Jesus, He will forgive you and
give you another chance. You are highly prized.

As Jesus comes through Jericho, Bartimaeus finds out who is causing this stir. He is blind, but his other senses are keen enough to know there is a crowd of people passing by. He is thirsty to change his condition. He does not allow the circumstance to keep him down. The people around him are trying to keep him in his place and make him keep quiet (Mk. 10:47–48). There are people in your life who want you to stay right where you are. They do not want you to change for the better. They are quick to tell you what you can and cannot do. And you may take their advice. There are churches that don't want to grow and expand to the people in their area. There is so much more that God wants to do in His churches but we do not allow the free moving of the Holy Spirit. Folk get satisfied with going to work, coming home, going to church, going home, going to work, coming home, going to church. For years, this is all most Christians do. Nothing has changed.

God wants some people who are hungry enough to fight through the criticism to do something different. Bartimaeus was tired of the same old thing. Day in and day out, they would take him out to the main highway to beg. Just think, no telling how much they charged for taking him to that location each day. He was thirsty for something else, and he knew Jesus could give him what he needed. If you want something different, you have to be thirsty. That thirst helps us to conquer our fears and enables us to see things we did not see before.

But the problem with us is that we are sometimes blind. We must develop a thirst and a vision for the things of Jesus Christ. Our blindness to the possibilities that await us in Jesus must be and can be overcome. In John chapter 4, the woman at the well was clueless about who Jesus is. She arrives to find a well sitting on a well, for Jesus is a well of everything we need. He is a well of resources that will supply all our needs. Jesus asked the women to give him a drink (Jn. 4:7–12). She did not know who Jesus was. Too many people do not know who Jesus is. Not only people outside the church but some people in the church do not know that Jesus is the same today as He was yesterday. Jesus has not changed. When you taste of the water Jesus gives, you will never thirst again. Your life will never be dry and parched. Your life will be overflowing. If your life is not overflowing, it maybe because you are blind and do not realize who Jesus is. You may not be thirsty enough. Thirst will cause you to seek after that which satisfies you.

But if you cannot see, it may be because religion can cause blindness. This woman told Jesus she was religious (Jn. 4:20). Jesus tells her that religion is about to change because God is going to be placed in her heart (Jn. 4:21–24). Then Jesus reveals Himself to her.

Jesus wants to reveal Himself to you today in areas of

your life that He has not touched. But you must be thirsty for a change in your life.

When Jesus called Bartimaeus to him, He asked him, "What do you want Me to do for you?" Bartimaeus could have asked for anything he wanted, but he asked for the very thing that kept him from being whole. He wanted his sight. Bartimaeus was thirsty for a change in his life (Mk. 10:51–52). He followed Jesus on the road.

# CHAPTER 7

## Sitting on the Sidelines of Life

Now they came to Jericho. As He went out of Jericho with His disciples and a great multitude, blind Bartimaeus, the son of Timaeus, sat by the road begging. And when he heard that it was Jesus of Nazareth, he began to cry out and say, "Jesus, Son of David, have mercy on me!" Then many warned him to be quiet; but he cried out all the more, "Son of David, have mercy on me!" So Jesus stood still and commanded him to be called. Then they called the blind man, saying to him, "Be of good cheer. Rise, He is calling you." And throwing aside his garment, he rose and came to Jesus. So Jesus answered and said to him, "What do you want Me to do for you?" The blind man said to Him, "Rabboni, that I may receive my sight." Then Jesus said to him,

"Go your way; your faith has made you well."
And immediately he received his sight and
followed Jesus on the road.

Mark 10:46–52

This blind man named Bartimaeus seems to have been dealt
a bad hand in life. He is blind and sitting on the side of the
road, begging. Sometimes life deals us a bad hand, but just
like playing cards, it is what we do with the hand we are dealt.
Regardless of what hand you have been dealt, today you are
a sum total of all the decisions you have made in life. You
can try to blame someone else, or you can take responsibility
for where you are today and move forward, but remember
there are consequences to each and every decision we make.
This is why we need to give thought to our decisions and
learn to respond to situations and not simply react. *Response*
occurs when we think things through, whatever decision
we must make, using our minds and sometimes getting
advice from others who are well informed, whereas *reactions*
are sometimes a reflex of our flesh or getting advice from
uninformed or unwise people. No matter what the situation
you find yourself in, God gives you the same thing He gives
someone who is rich, poor, Black, Brown, Asian or White,
and that is twenty-four hours each day. It is what we do with
these twenty-four hours that can make us or break us.

Each morning we can start new. Lamentations 3:22–24 (HCSB) says, "Because of the LORD's faithful love we do not perish, for His mercies never end. They are new every morning; great is Your faithfulness! I say: The LORD is my portion; therefore, I will put my hope in Him." This is very important because we all are given a new opportunity each day.

Suppose someone has decided to put 8,640 pennies in your bank account each day. They will give the pennies to you each day, but you must spend them all the day you get them. You cannot carry a penny over to the next day. If you do, the pennies will stop coming. You must spend $86.40 each day or $604.80 a week, for a total of $31,449.60 per year. This is what you must spend in order to keep the pennies coming. The number of pennies in my example equals the number of seconds in each day that God gives you, every week and every year. The question for you is, *How are you spending your day?*

In our text, we find Bartimaeus spending his day sitting on the side of the road and begging. We are never told how long he's been sitting there or whether this was his daily routine. We just find him on this day begging on the side of the road. We only know a couple of things about his condition from this text. First, he is blind. Second, he is in need because he is begging for money. Third, he is Timaeus's son. Fourth, he is outside the city of Jericho.

Let's look at his first condition, blindness. There was no braille for him to scan with his fingers, so he could not get a job that required literacy, and we do not know if he could play a musical instrument and sing like the great musicians Stevie Wonder, Ray Charles, Ronnie Millsap, or so many other talented blind people we know. So Bartimaeus's work and job opportunities were limited: his job was to sit on the side of the road and beg.

We all have observed people begging on the side of the road. When my wife and I were visiting New Orleans, we were amazed to see so many people finding different ways of making money. There was a guy who just stood on a make-believe ladder that seemed to have no support. There was another person painted in silver in a frozen stance, and another playing the saxophone. So many more were doing odd things, but they all had a donation bucket for visitors and observers to drop money into. They, in a sense, were sitting on the sidelines—begging, if you would—but they all seemed to be in good physical condition and could have held down a job or do something else with their lives. They were providing entertainment, but just sitting on the sidelines doing nothing but begging and wanting people to give them money and not working for it is what some people do as their job.

You may find yourself in this same situation as Bartimaeus, handicapped in one area of your life that affects your whole life and in need of something beyond your reach. Your need may differ from the person beside you or the person next door and even from the person doing your same job. Your need is specific to you. You don't have to be poor or blind to have a need. You can be middle class or wealthy, you may be employed, you may be upper management or own a business. You may be a student. You may be married, divorced, or single—but you still have a need that needs to be met. There is something unfulfilled in your life. Sometimes others don't understand your situation, but you know what is handicapping you. Your need, your desire, is real.

Too many times people will be asking why or how you got in the water while you are drowning instead of throwing you a rope to get you out. You may be hurting this day and just need to know someone cares about you. You may have been seeking answers to your problems and can't get any. Your circumstances have not changed, and you find yourself on the sidelines of life. It may be psychological, it may be spiritual, or it may be physical, but you are not able to get into the mainstream of life or into other things that you desire. You are relegated to the sidelines of life, watching others pass you by. You have been taking two steps, but it feels like life is pushing you back three steps. You have resolved in your mind to just settle for the sidelines of life while others seem to pass you by.

Too many times we get jealous, we get envious, and we

get covetous of other people who are passing us by, and we began to dwell too long on our condition and want others to have pity on us. So we settle for a handout, and it becomes a lifestyle or daily routine without our realizing that we need a hand up, not a hand out, to get out of our condition. You must settle down and remember "what God does for others He can do for me." If we don't, we can become just like Bartimaeus was at the beginning of the story, blind.

Being blind to all life's possibilities is when you are not able to see your way through your situation. Your vision is limited. Are you sitting on the sidelines of your situation without a vision for the future? You have no idea what you may be doing ten years from now? You have no plan to change your situation, and no vision to see your way out? I have learned that the person who has no targets in life to shoot for will miss the mark every time. I am here to tell you that even though Bartimaeus had no sight, he still had a vision for his future.

There is an answer to your problem today. Look at Exodus 4:2 (NKJV): "So the Lord said to him, 'What is that in your hand?' He said, "a rod." God asked Moses this question, and Moses thought it was just a rod. He did not realize it represented God's power in his hand. Just like Moses knew how to use the rod in his hand to guide the sheep, but God was training him to guide His people out of Egypt. You too have something in your possession that God wants to use.

Look at David in 1 Samuel 17:40 (NKJV):

> Then he took his staff in his hand; and he
> chose for himself five smooth stones from the
> brook, and put them in a shepherd's bag, in a
> pouch which he had, and his sling was in his
> hand. And he drew near to the Philistine.

David knew how to use a sling. It never occurred to him while keeping sheep and using his sling that one day he would save Israel from its enemies with that same sling. David was elevated from shepherding sheep to shepherding God's people. What do you have in your possession that will change your situation?

Now let us go back to our text, Mark 10:47 (NKJV): "And when he heard that it was Jesus of Nazareth, he began to cry out and say, 'Jesus, Son of David, have mercy on me!'" Bartimaeus had no sight, but he had a voice, and he used what he had to cry out to Jesus, *"Son of David, Have mercy on me!"* The more people told him to be quiet, the more he used what he had. If you are going to change your situation you have to use what you have in your possession. You have got to quit cursing the darkness in your life and light a candle; in other words, you must learn to use what is in your hand. It may be your talents, your gifts, or your expertise. Or it may just be your voice. Just give it to God, and let God guide you through.

When you learn to use what God has placed in your possession, you will never judge your future on your present situation. You will begin to move from the sidelines of life to the mainstream of God's flowing. If you are to move from beggar to giver, you will find out why it is more blessed to give than receive. If you have the gift of selling and move from being a dope dealer to being a car salesman, God will drive you in another direction in life. If you move from being strung out on alcohol or drugs to being high on Jesus, He can make you walk straight. You must make a change in your life by taking advantage of every opportunity that presents itself to you.

During my jail ministry and preaching in the local jail, I had an inmate to tell me he could get out of jail if he had a job, but he stated that he was not going work at a hamburger place to flip burgers, so he decided to do all his time and stay in jail. I told him if he would go learn how they ordered the burgers and how they mixed the special sauce and what buns they use, in a few years he could be flipping burgers for himself at his own restaurant. His name was Tommy, and I told him he could name it McTommy's. We must learn to recognize and take advantage of opportunities that come our way, no matter how small. We must use what is available to us as long as it glorifies the Lord.

There must be a decision made in your life to change your situation. If you are just as broke today as you were five years ago or ten years ago, add up all the money that has run through your hands and see how you have handled it. God wants you to learn how to use what you have in your hand.

Look at Bartimaeus's position. He is on the sidelines, and a few feet away are people in the main flow of life, on the way to the place of God. It is a paradox to be so close to the flow of things yet be so far away. My wife was visiting Durbin, South Africa, but had not learned anything about South Africa before going. She had her image of Africa in her mind already. So when she saw the city of Durbin, she was impressed. Then the tour bus drove out of town just a few miles, and she saw the Africa that was in her mind. She could not believe how a beautiful city, with all the modern things, can be so close to a shanty town that is the opposite of Durbin. Yet that seems to be the norm. I told my wife she did not have to go to South Africa to see this: just look at most cities here in the United States. Just a few blocks from a pristine downtown in most cities are neighborhoods and areas that are very depressed. This same condition exists for a lot of people—so close to success yet so far away from it, sitting on the sidelines of life but close to the mainstream of life.

Now you must make a change in your life. Jesus is standing still for you today. He wants to get you off the sidelines of life and put you in the mainstream of things. Jesus is calling you into something new in your life. You have survived where you have been; now let Jesus anoint you to where He wants to take you. Jesus will answer your request to change you to what He is calling you into. Jesus has anointed you to get off the sidelines of life and to move into the flow of life and live more abundantly. You must know that the power within you is greater than the task ahead of you: "Greater is He who is in you the he that is in the world" (1 Jn. 4:4 KJV).

Jesus is standing still to move you out of your yesterdays into a bright tomorrow and a terrific right now. Jesus is calling you into the mainstream of life; it is time for you to accept His invitation. There are talents and gifts deep inside you that must come out—that new business, that new degree, that new house or new job. Get off the sidelines of life and flow with Jesus in the mainstream of things, because He came to give you life and live more abundantly.

# CHAPTER 8

## Leaving All to Follow Jesus

Now they came to Jericho. As He went out of Jericho with His disciples and a great multitude, blind Bartimaeus, the son of Timaeus, sat by the road begging. And when he heard that it was Jesus of Nazareth, he began to cry out and say, "Jesus, Son of David, have mercy on me!" Then many warned him to be quiet; but he cried out all the more, "Son of David, have mercy on me!" So Jesus stood still and commanded him to be called. Then they called the blind man, saying to him, "Be of good cheer. Rise, He is calling you." And throwing aside his garment, he rose and came to Jesus. So Jesus answered and said to him, "What do you want Me to do for you?" The blind man said to Him, "Rabboni, that I may receive my sight." Then Jesus said to him,

"Go your way; your faith has made you well."
And immediately he received his sight and
followed Jesus on the road."

Mark 10: 46–52 NKJV

During the pandemic of 2020–2021, we all have learned some things that will shape our lives in the future. It is in trying times that you learn who you can depend on and who you cannot depend on. We all have been challenged, and I pray that we learn to stand up for our faith and for our families and friends and that we continue to support our churches during these trying times. It is these trying times that will show where we are spiritually and mentally and in other areas of our lives, as our faith is challenged again and again. There are family problems that have surfaced; husband and wives, children and parents, and so many other relationships have been put to the test, not to mention all the financial problems that have arisen. I don't know about you, but times were dark enough in America in 2020, and we are due for a change as we hear all the numbers of people who are dying from this coronavirus. "Jesus, we need you to come by and rescue us from ourselves."

In our text, Jesus is on the way to Jerusalem for the last time. It is at this visit to Jerusalem that Jesus is to be crucified and on the third day raised up. So as he passes through the city of Jericho, there is a blind man named Bartimaeus who realizes something is happening. Even though he cannot see, he senses a difference in the crowd noise. He may not be able to see, but he can hear. You see, you cannot let one defect in your life affect the rest of your life. You cannot let one problem become the problem.

I will make three points here.

**1. You must be an overcomer.** "And when he heard that it was Jesus of Nazareth, he began to cry out and say, 'Jesus, Son of David, have mercy on me!'" (Mk.10:47). We are never told how long this man has been in this condition; we have no other information about him except his daddy's name is Timaeus. We are told that those around him are telling him to be quiet. But the more he is told to be quiet, the more he yells out to Jesus. You must realize there are people in your life who do not want you to change. They will tell you how bad your ideas are; they will ridicule you behind your back and sometimes to your face. And all the while they will draw all the life out of you, to the point that it all becomes a routine. Life can become so systemic or systematic that you begin to think that this is the way life for you *should* be. And you will pass that way of life on to your children. You can pray all day and night, but until you apply God's word after you say amen and the prayer is over, your situation will stay the same.

There are some things we must do for ourselves.

Bartimaeus was not going to let his condition nor his past dictate to him his future. He did not let his family connections dictate his future. His father, Timaeus, must have been known, or maybe had a reputation that stood out. Nevertheless, Bartimaeus wanted a change in his life.

I am reminded of the story in John chapter 5 and the question that Jesus asked of the man who had an infirmity for thirty-eight years: "Do you want to be made well?" He asked only to get this man to start thinking about his situation, because too many times we just settle for where we are in life and never stretch ourselves to become more than what others think we can be.

Bartimaeus knew that a change in his life was coming. He used what he had, and that was his ability to hear. Not only did he hear the crowd, he had heard about Jesus, because he called Him "Jesus, Son of David" several times. Bartimaeus used what he had—his mouth—to get Jesus's attention. What do you have in your possession? Yes, you have something. *You must be an overcomer.*

**2. You have something within waiting to come out that others do not see.** "Then many warned him to be quiet; but he cried out all the more, 'Son of David, have mercy on me!'" (Mk. 10:48). Bartimaeus did not let what others saw in him affect what he saw in himself; regardless of whether he could see, he had a vision for his future. So many times, I meet people who are not living up to their potential—they never even realize they have potential within, bursting to be exposed. So many times, I see people just accepting bad circumstances in their lives and never moving past where they are in life. They never were told they have the power within to change a generation so their children and grandchildren will not have to travel the same path they have traveled.

When I go to a funeral, then on to the graveyard and where I see all the graves, I think of all the songs that were not written, all the paintings that were not painted, all the businesses that were not started, all the inventions that have not been invented, all the money that has not been made, all the discoveries that were not discovered. I look out over the graves and realize that the cemetery is the richest place in any city, full of unfulfilled dreams, unfulfilled hopes, and unfulfilled joys. That is what is sad about a cemetery, because it is so rich.

You have something in your possession that God has given you. These people around Bartimaeus kept telling him to be quiet, but the more they said be quiet, the more he cried out "Son of David, have mercy on me!" There must be a cry from deep inside of you to Jesus. There are people around you that want to keep you in your situation and circumstances, but change is left entirely up to you.

We are the sum total of our life's decisions. We are where we are today because of the decisions we have made. Jesus says in Matthew 15:8 (NKJV), "These people draw near to

Me with their mouth, and honor Me with their lips, but their heart is far from Me." If you do nothing else during this pandemic, get serious about your relationship with Jesus. Move from religion to relationship. Why? You have something within waiting to come out that others do not see. Only in the presence of Jesus can it come out!

**3. Jesus says, "What do you want Me to do for you?"** "So Jesus answered and said to him, 'What do you want Me to do for you?' The blind man said to Him, 'Rabboni, that I may receive my sight'" (Mk. 10:51). Bartimaeus had an answer: "that I may receive my sight." Bartimaeus knew what he needed, and he knew what to do after he got what he needed. Please understand that what is *wanted* is not always what is *needed*. You must be able to distinguish between the two. He was begging on the side of the road, and he was there to get money, but was the money he's getting enough to sustain him or change his lifestyle? But if he received his sight, the possibilities of living his dreams, fulfilling life's promises, and reaching his potential were now in his grasp.

It is good that we feed and clothe people here at New Beginnings Christian Ministries and at other churches and nonprofit charities, but until we move to addressing the cause of people being hungry, we cannot pat ourselves on the back. They will continue to want us to feed them and to need clothing and shelter, and we and other ministries will continue to try to fill that need and want. We who are pro-life must be pro-life from birth to death and care about a person's life their *whole* life, not just about a birth.

There are people who do not know how to answer the question Jesus asked Bartimaeus: "What do you want Me to do for you?" We must convince them that an encounter with Jesus is life-changing, and that is what is needed in people's lives. Now look again at Bartimaeus's encounter with Jesus: he gets what he needs. Then he follows Jesus on the way or on the road to Jerusalem. You must be willing to change your position in life when Jesus gives you what you need. You may need to change friends; you will definitely need to remove some people from your life. And you must get ready for people to start hating on you because you have changed for the better.

Then most of all, you must start following Jesus in His way. Study His word and become a doer of the Word. Apply God's principles to your life, and grasp what Matthew 6:33 says: "But seek first the kingdom of God and His righteousness, and all these things shall be added to you."

If you are reading this and have not fulfilled your dreams, do not go to the grave with unfulfilled dreams. Learn to leave it all here before you die. Leave this world empty because you have poured it all out for Jesus while living on this side of heaven. Be all God has intended you to be. Live life on purpose. Leave it all to follow Jesus. Jesus is the way, the truth, and the life. His name is Jesus.

Jesus says in Matthew 11:28–30 (NKJV): "Come to Him, all who labor and are heavy laden, and He will give you rest. Take My yoke upon you and learn from Me, for I am gentle and lowly in heart and you will find rest for your souls, For My yoke is easy and My burden is light." Leave your situation and learn to follow Jesus regardless of what others around you say or try to do against you as you respond to "What do you want Me to do for you?"

Proverbs 18:21 (NKJV) says, "Death and life are in the power of the tongue, and those who love it will eat its fruit." The ball of life is in your court, and the decision for your future lies in your hand. Isn't it time do live the way Jesus directs you to, and to learn that leaving all to follow Jesus is the best way for you?

# CHAPTER 9

## Can You Ask Jesus, "What Do You Want Me to Do for You?"

So Jesus answered and said to him, "What do you want Me to do for you?" The blind man said to Him, "Rabboni, that I may receive my sight." Then Jesus said to him, "Go your way; your faith has made you well." And immediately he received his sight and followed Jesus on the road.

Mark 10:51–52

One of the stated purposes of our ministry at New Beginnings Christian Ministries is to "bring the good news of Jesus Christ, the risen savior, to the people of South Central Kentucky and the world. To offer people a personal relationship with Jesus, to make disciples of Christ, and to empower people through the knowledge of the Word of God by changing lives, restoring and strengthening families, and seeing people set free." We add, "making disciples and reproducing after Christ." It is our desire at New Beginnings to help people we come in contact with through this ministry and to move them in this direction. The body of Christ, the church, must develop disciples of Christ; we must all be challenged to move toward being Christlike. We must become Christ in the world to shine in the dark and dim places we encounter in our daily lives. The Kingdom of Heaven has been ushered in, and we must tell everybody about Jesus and His love.

In our text is a blind man named Bartimaeus, and Jesus is asking him "What do you want Me to do for you?" Jesus's ministry on this earth was an example we are to continue. In fact, when someone asks me to define what a church is, I can give the meaning of the Greek word *ekklesia*. From the Strong's Dictionary, this word is a feminine noun which means "the called people or those called out or assembled in the public affairs of a free state, the body of free citizens called together by a herald." But I would rather give the meaning I have arrived at, which is a body of baptized believers of Jesus Christ, called out and called into the service of Christ to continue the work of Jesus. The emphasis on continuation puts the church in a position of developing people after Christ, as Jesus Himself says in John 14:12–14 "Most assuredly, I say to you, he who believes in Me, the works that I do he will do also; and greater *works* than these he will do, because I go to My Father. [13] And whatever you ask in My name, that I will do, that the Father may be glorified in the Son. [14] If you ask anything in My name, I will do *it.*" We are the ones who should be posing the question "What do you want me to do for you?" to those who are in need.

We must learn from the example Jesus gave in John 12:24–26 Most assuredly, I say to you, unless a grain of wheat falls into the ground and dies, it remains alone; but if it dies, it produces much grain. [25] He who loves his life will lose it, and he who hates his life in this world will keep it for eternal life. [26] If anyone serves Me, let him follow Me; and where I am, there My servant will be also. If anyone serves Me, him *My* Father will honor. Here Jesus unlocks and reveals to us God's eternal operation on earth in the work of sowing and reaping. When we unlock God's eternal operation and allow it to flow in our lives, things begin to change. In Genesis 1:11–12, God set in motion sowing and reaping. We are told in Galatians 6:7–10 not to give up when we sow, as a harvest will come. There is a law of the harvest or a law of our sowing that cannot be broken.

**1. We reap what we sow.** This is a law of likeness. If you sow weeds, you are going to get a harvest of weeds. If you sow thistle seed, you will get a thistle bush every time. It will never fail, even if you sow a million seeds—you will always get what is sown. The quality of that which is sown is bound inextricably to the quality of that which is reaped. There is a locked-in likeness that guarantees against variation.

The same principle works in the spiritual realm. You and I, like the seed, have an indwelling life system dominating us, whether it is the life of Christ or that of the Devil. It is life's circumstances that bring us opportunities to allow the life force within to burst forth with its inner life-giving power. If we allow the power of God to burst forth and dominate us, then we have life and live more abundantly (Jn. 10:10). If we allow the enemy to dominate us, then we reap death. But when we consent to be planted to His glory and be on display to show His indwelling life, the life He planted within us will burst forth.

It is the same when we give: we will get in return the same quality. We will get what we sow. If we sow trouble, discord, discontent, and a negative attitude, we will reap a bumper crop pf that. If we sow love, joy, happiness, and a positive attitude, we can expect to be showered with it. We reap what we sow!

**2. But we can reap more than we sow.** Reaping more than we sow is what makes the law of the harvest profitable. It is the multiplication part of the law. There would be no future in sowing if we did not reap a harvest greater than the quantity of the seed sown. This multiplication is greater when we sow in fertile soil (Matt. 13:1–8). If you fail to watch or to be careful where you sow, your harvest may not come up, and all the cultivating in the world serves no purpose in compensating for the failure to sow. Where nothing is sown, nothing is reaped. Where something is sown, something is reaped—and it is always much more. The law of the harvest is operative not only in the physical realm but in the spiritual realm. The physical is only a picture of the spiritual. If sowing in the physical realm reaps rich dividends, then why not in the spiritual? God controls it all (Rom. 1:20).

**3. You reap later than you sow.** The nature of the life within the seed includes a timeline that cannot be circumvented. We have to respect and go along with its laws. The harvest is always later than the sowing. The more we learn about the nature of the particular life cycle, the better we can cooperate with it to produce a greater harvest. In the spiritual realm, there is a life cycle waiting to burst out upon our world. It is in us and includes all the gifts and talents that have been entrusted to us. When we begin to line up and apply God's word in our lives and to cooperate to the best of our ability with that life cycle, dynamic things happen. The harvest always comes later and abundantly.

Jesus tells us in Luke 6:38 (NKJV):

> Give and it will be given to you; good measure, pressed down, shaken together, and running over will be put into your bosom. For with

the same measure that you use, it will be measured back to you."

Jesus never tells you what to give; He just says "give." Too many times we think it is just money, but Jesus wants you to give your talents, your time, and your gifts to the work of the Kingdom. It does not matter what others do to you. Romans 12:19–20 (NKJV) says:

> Do not avenge yourselves, but rather give place to wrath: for it is written, Vengeance is Mine, I will repay, says the Lord. Therefore, if your enemy is hungry, feed him; if he is thirsty, give him a drink; for in so doing, you will heap coals of fire on his head.

There is one more scripture I want to share that unlocked some things for me, and that is Ephesians 6:8 (NKJV), "knowing that whatever good anyone does, he will receive the same from the Lord, whether he is a slave or free." The Ron Whitlock version is "To those whom God is a blessing *to*, He is a blessing *through*." Are you ready to ask Jesus, "What do you want me to do for you?"

# CHAPTER 10

## Wor(k)ship

Now they came to Jericho. As He went out of Jericho with His disciples and a great multitude, blind Bartimaeus, the son of Timaeus, sat by the road begging. And when he heard that it was Jesus of Nazareth, he began to cry out and say, "Jesus, Son of David, have mercy on me!" Then many warned him to be quiet; but he cried out all the more, "Son of David, have mercy on me!" So Jesus stood still and commanded him to be called. Then they called the blind man, saying to him, "Be of good cheer. Rise, He is calling you." And throwing aside his garment, he rose and came to Jesus. So Jesus answered and said to him, "What do you want Me to do for you?" The blind man said to Him, "Rabboni, that I may receive my sight." Then Jesus said to him,

"Go your way; your faith has made you well."
And immediately he received his sight and
followed Jesus on the road.

Mark 10:46–52

One of the most important things that we get involved with in our church services is worship. The songs, the scriptures recited, the testimonies, and other activities we are involved in or observe during worship really set the tone for the preached word. But there is another side of our participation that many do not move into. That is the side of our Christian walk called *service*. The service side of our Christian walk is the work of Christianity, and it is the part that others see in us and that the world is looking for in all Christians. This side of the Christian walk—that is, the *work* we do as Christians—takes time to learn and to operate in.

Ephesians 2:10 says, "For we are His workmanship, created in Christ Jesus for good works, which God prepared beforehand that we should walk in them." As I studied the words work and *worship*, I came up with a word that combines both of these: *workship*. (This is a made-up word that you will not find in the dictionary. I learned to make up words from Dr. Walter Malone, pastor of Canaan Christian Church in Louisville, Kentucky.) I define *workship* as "the application of biblical principles when transitioning from the praise and worship of God to doing the work of God, letting others see the attributes of God at work in your life."

One of the saddest things that happens in our churches is the lack of change that occurs in people's lives. The question is, How to win others to Jesus if there is no change in your life? People know how to be "churchie." We know the right things to say in church. We know how to put on our church act while in church. We know the church phases and titles to use when addressing others while in church. That's what it means to be "churchie." But when it comes to things people see in you every day, it is not your hair nor the new clothes you wear but an overall change in your life that will draw others to Jesus.

Regardless of where you are in your walk with Jesus, or even if you have not accepted Him as your personal savior, Jesus will meet you where you are in life. In our text, Jesus meets a man named Bartimaeus, who is blind and begging on the side of the road. He did not go and change clothes or put on sunglasses when Jesus showed up. He met Jesus just as he was. You always want Jesus to meet you where you are. Never mask yourself, never cover your problem; let your struggle be seen. Your situation, your habit, your faults and failures—let it all be seen by Jesus. Always allow Jesus to meet you where you are. Be willing to take off your mask when standing before Jesus.

Whenever you decide that you have had enough, you

need to cry out to Jesus. Cry out to Him just as Bartimaeus does in verse 47: "And when he heard that it was Jesus of Nazareth, he began to cry out and say, 'Jesus, Son of David, have mercy on me!'" Bartimaeus could not see Jesus, but he could hear it was Jesus. Bartimaeus used what he had, his ears and he heard it was Jesus. You must begin your work as a Christian by learning to use what you have at your disposal. We always get God's blessing when we use what we have, as with the rod of Moses or the slingshot of David.

Bartimaeus called out and praised Jesus as the "Son of David." I don't know about you, but I find praise will open doors when nothing else will help. I dare you to praise God through your tears, praise Him through your setbacks and setups, praise Him through your failures and mistakes. I dare you to get on your knees and call on the name of Jesus. Stop your crying and start a high praise. Get your praise on. It is no one else's business—it is between you and Jesus. Verse 48 says, "Then many warned him to be quiet; but he cried out all the more, 'Son of David, have mercy on me!'" There are people in your life who do not want to see you change. They will tell you to be quiet when you are about to get your breakthrough!

Bartimaeus's transformation started when he began to call and praise Jesus for being the Son of David, the promised Messiah whose kingdom would never end. Transformation in your life starts when you hook up with Jesus's purpose.

Quit wanting Jesus to hook up with *your* purpose, *your* ministry, *your* this and that. Hook up with Jesus's purpose, and He will lead you to your purpose in Him. He is the Son of David, and His kingdom has no end.

We are never told how Bartimaeus got on the side of the road. Did Bartimaeus pay Uber or the local cab company to drop him off? A food truck may have been there selling Reuben sandwiches and just waiting for his order. The local tax collector was probably nearby to get a cut of the money blind Bartimaeus collected. In other words, there were people benefiting from Bartimaeus's condition. There are people in your life who benefit from your condition, and they do not want to see a change in your life. What, the bank is going to give me no-interest credit for ninety days? What, buy one, get one free? What, I got to have that new phone so I can google? People benefit from your problems, but Jesus is coming and calling your name because you are willing to show Him all your faults and failures that you cannot show anyone else.

If you do not get anything else out of this chapter, get this: **Jesus cannot put you back together unless He has all the broken pieces.** No matter how painful it is, no matter how embarrassing it is, no matter who gets upset with you telling your faults and failures to Jesus, and no matter what it may cost you, give it all to Jesus. Bartimaeus did not care what others thought; he just kept on calling on "Jesus, Son of David, have mercy on me!" When we call Jesus with a sincere heart, we get His attention and He responds, as in verses 49–50: "So Jesus stood still and commanded him to be called. Then they called the blind man, saying to him, 'Be of good cheer. Rise, He is calling you.' And throwing aside his garment, he rose and came to Jesus." We must be willing to throw away everything that identified us with our past. We must be willing to change everything in our life that we can in order to get to Jesus and get that spiritual change that changes us physically, so that our friends can see a change in us.

What are you still holding on to that keeps you bogged down in your past? Is it unforgiveness? Is it self-pity? Is it somebody you should have let go years ago, or a job or career that wouldn't allow you to go in another direction? Is it getting off welfare and getting a job? Let it go, throw it aside—Jesus is calling you to Him.

In verse 51, Jesus asks Bartimaeus a question. Are you ready to answer the question that Jesus is asking you? Bartimaeus was ready—he knew just how to answer the question. Have you taken time to assess your situation in life so you will know exactly what you really need? Bartimaeus had heard about Jesus, and Bartimaeus knew scripture, as he called Jesus the Son of David. Bartimaeus did not care what others thought of him. Are you ready to answer Jesus's question?

It is when we are able to answer the question that we

move from worship to work. We move into *workship*. We move from Sunday worship to everyday working for Jesus everywhere we are. We move out of the four walls of the church to go where Jesus goes, as Bartimaeus does in verse 52: "Then Jesus said to him, 'Go your way; your faith has made you well.' And immediately he received his sight and followed Jesus on the road." Jesus commands us to *go*. It is when we act on our faith that we get our vision, our purpose, and our assignment, and we move into workship.

It is time for people to see a new you instead of a new ride. It is time for people to see a new you instead of a new dress. It is time for people to see a new you instead of a new expensive pair of shoes. There is nothing wrong with having things, but you need to quit allowing things to have you. Who are you really trying to impress? Those you are trying to impress are not paying attention to you anyway. It is time to focus on Jesus, the Alpha and Omega, the beginning and the end. Jesus, the Lilly of the Valley, the Rose of Sharon. His name is Jesus. Our text says Bartimaeus heard it was Jesus of Nazareth, and you see rumor become reality.

When I was growing up, I used to hear my mother talk about Jesus. Momma would say, "Jesus will make a way out of no way." I am one of thirteen children. I have six sisters and six brothers, and a mother who trusted God and knew Jesus. She testified often, but what she was saying was only a rumor to me. But one day in Louisville, Kentucky, I found myself in a bad place in life, and I needed a change. I had been in church all my life, but on this day I really called on Jesus—and He showed up and He showed out in my life. He moved me from rumor to reality. Some people have heard of Jesus, but until you try Him for yourself, He will only be a rumor.

People need to know that Jesus conquered death, hell, and the grave. He rose up with all power in His hands. When He conquers your problem, you move from rumor to reality, from worship to *workship*. Jesus healed Bartimaeus of his blindness. And if you are blind to the fact that Jesus is the Son of God, He can make you see who He is. Jesus cleansed ten lepers; Jesus healed a man at the pool of Bethesda who was in a bad condition for thirty-eight years. I find no fault in Him. Jesus healed Peter's mother-in-law and a woman with an issue of blood for twelve long years. He raised Jairus's daughter and healed a man with a withered hand. I find no fault in Him. He walked on water, turned water into wine, and calmed a raging sea when they woke Him up from the bottom of the boat. I have tried Him and I find no fault in Him.

Call on Him as Bartimaeus did ("Jesus, Son of David, have mercy on me"), and you will begin to see Him as Bartimaeus saw Him. You will see in Him completeness, you will see in Him wholeness, you will see in Him health, you will see in Him peace, you will see in Him safety, you will see in Him soundness, you will see in Him tranquility, you will see in Him prosperity, you will see in Him perfectness, you will see in Him fullness, you will see in Him rest and harmony. Try Him for yourself, and you will see yourself move from worship to WORKSHIP.

# CHAPTER 11

## Move of Faith

When we accept Jesus as our personal savior, it is through faith and God's grace. So as we start our walk with Jesus, it is a walk of faith. We are told in Rom.1:17 (NKJV), "the Just shall live by faith," which means our faith walk is 24/7. I have noticed that when our faith is questioned, or when we are put in a position to use our faith, we say, "I have faith that God will ..." or "I'm praying for God to ... I have faith in His Word." We say, "God's Word says this" ... or "I'm trusting in His Word." We then wait until we see His Word manifest in our circumstance. Praise God!

But now God wants to move us to another level of faith that we have never experienced in our lives. He allows situations and circumstances to arise in our lives that cause us to rely on faith to get through. In searching scriptures that will help us all move to that next level of our walk of faith, I'm brought to the Gospel of Mark. I credit Dr. Charles

Baker for demanding and challenging me to always verify things by searching the scriptures.

Mark's gospel was written to show Jesus as a servant, with an emphasis on His miracles. Mark focuses on Jesus as a servant who ministers to the physical and spiritual needs of others. As I have studied Mark and continue to study this gospel, I find how fast-moving Marks shows Jesus to be. We find the phases "and Jesus," "again He," "and He said," and "immediately." We also see the word "then" several times in this book. In other words, Mark shows Jesus always on the move, performing one miracle after another, sharing one parable after another, visiting one city after another as he goes from place to place. Mark moves so fast in this gospel that he hardly mentions anyone's name outside of Jesus's disciples. Mark does not take time to mention the people's names that Jesus encounters.

But in verses 46–51 of chapter 10, Mark writes things that go against his writing style. First, he mentions Bartimaeus by name and his father, Timaeus. This gets my attention. To me it sticks out like a thumb on a hand of fingers. No one else in scripture mentions Bartimaeus's name; nowhere in scripture can you find Bartimaeus except here in the Gospel of Mark.

Second, as we observe Mark's fast pace in showing how Jesus moves from one scene to another and from place to place, in verse 49 Mark says that Jesus stood still. After showing how quickly Jesus moves from place to place, now

Mark writes, "So Jesus stood still." So I ask myself two questions. Why did Mark mention Bartimaeus by name, and why did Jesus stand still? In trying to answer these questions, I have concluded that there was something so powerful in this story that I needed to dig deeper to uncover what only the Holy Spirit can reveal and make obvious to the spiritual eye. Here is what God has revealed to me.

It was a Jewish custom for beggars to place themselves on the busiest traveled path, just as today we see people with signs asking for money only at busy intersections in our city. They will hold up signs saying "need money homeless" or "will work for money" and so on. We identify them by their signs, but in Jesus's day beggars wore clothing that identified them. But they too chose the busiest thoroughfares to position themselves in. Many Jews met in Jericho before traveling to Jerusalem for Passover celebrations, so the road leaving Jericho became a popular spot for beggars. But on this day it is Jesus who is traveling up the highway, on His way to Jerusalem for the last time. This brings me to my first point.

**1. Our faith in Jesus causes us to change identity.** Bartimaeus's garment was much more than a piece of cloth used to collect money. It was his identity. But in verse 50, "and throwing aside his garment, he rose and came to Jesus." Everyone knew he was a beggar by the garment. It labeled him. So when coming to Jesus, we must be willing to lose the identity the world has given us. Galatians 2:20 (NKJV) says, "I have been crucified with Christ; it is no longer I who live, but Christ liven in me; and the life which I now live in the flesh I live by faith in the Son of God, who loved me and gave Himself for me." We also must lose the beggar's mentality that says "you don't belong," just as Bartimaeus sitting on the side of the road was told to keep quiet.

Many times, the enemy tries to convince us that we don't belong and might as well stop calling out because Jesus is just passing us by and is not concerned with us. But the mentality of the children is to say "we belong"—we are heirs of God and joint-heirs with Christ. Romans 8:17 (NKJV) says, "and if children, then heirs--heirs of God and joint heirs with Christ, if indeed we suffer with Him, that we may also be glorified together." Cast away the beggar's garment today, and realize you are a new creature, a child of God who belongs and is loved!

**2. Our faith in Jesus gives us boldness.** With all the people telling Bartimaeus to be quiet, he had a boldness to approach Jesus: "And throwing aside his garment, he rose and came to Jesus." Hebrews 4:16 (NKJV) says, "Let us therefore come boldly to the throne of grace, that we may obtain mercy and find grace to help in time of need." Our faith must grow to a point in our lives that causes us to be bold. Our faith requires vision beyond what we see. The vision I am talking about is not merely seeing with your eyes but is a prophetical seeing into your destiny. God is calling me to speak into many people's lives that I may never meet. My faith is going to take to places I never thought I would go and cause me to do things for God I never thought I would do. Where is your faith taking you?

**3. Your faith must cause you to have a vision that is seen by those around you.** In verse 49, Jesus stands still because He knows this is not someone who just wants His autograph or a photo op—Bartimaeus has faith, and Jesus knows it. Jesus had seen great faith in a Roman centurion and a Phoenician woman whose daughter had an unclean spirit, but this blind man's act of faith caused Jesus to stop and be still and to call for him to come. Then Bartimaeus did an act of faith by throwing away the garment that identified him as a beggar. The discarding of his uniform was an act of faith on his part in trusting that he would no longer need it. Bartimaeus had vision—he just could not see physically. He could visualize himself walking with Jesus.

Bartimaeus had a vision even before Jesus showed up that day. He must have heard about the man who went and washed in the pool of Siloam after Jesus put spit on the ground and made clay then put it on his eyes. When Bartimaeus got his sight, he followed Jesus in the way. Notice that the road that Jesus took was the road to Jerusalem—and the cross! Bartimaeus was one of the few followers of Jesus who was ready to follow Him all the way to the cross.

Your faith must be at a point where you are willing to die to self and live for Jesus. Jesus *stood still* because He knew what Bartimaeus would do when his move of faith was granted. Jesus knew Bartimaeus would follow Him all the way to the cross. Is your move of faith causing Jesus to stand still? Is Jesus confident enough in you that He will ask, "What do you want Me to do for you?" Is your prayer not being answered because Jesus knows what you will do if He grants you what you want? Are you the center of your world, and not Jesus?

If you want Jesus to bless your ministry, your ideas, your family, and your goals in life, put Jesus in the center of your life. Jesus knows if you are going to follow Him in the way. If you die to self and are willing to change your identity and follow Jesus in the way, then Jesus will stand still for you because of your move of faith and grant your heart's desire. Faith in the gospel produces *power*. Believing is one of the most powerful fundamental principles at the heart of Christianity. The content of the gospel is power: power to produce miracles, power to change lives, power to heal, power to deliver the oppressed, and power to enable the failing person to live a successful, victorious life. Any person can unlock this power through believing the gospel and acting on faith.

It is time for you to have faith in the Son, the Bright and Morning Star, the Light of the World. He is the Good

Shepherd, the True Vine, the Lily of the Valley, the Rose of Sharon, the King of the Jews, the Lamb of God, the Way, the Truth, the Life—the only way to the Father. His name is Jesus, my mountain mover:

> Most assuredly, I say to you, he who believes in Me, the works that I do he will do also; and greater works than these he will do, because I go to My Father. And whatever you ask in My name, that I will do, that the Father may be glorified in the Son. If you ask anything in My name, I will do it. (Jn. 14:12–14 NKJV)

It is when you begin to speak God's Word, no matter what the circumstances are, and begin to walk in faith that you are empowered to create change. Change happens when you act on faith regardless of what someone else says or no matter what the circumstances are. You are walking by faith and not by sight, and in believing you see the goodness of the Lord in the land of the living. Do as Bartimaeus did: start a move of faith before it appears. Bartimaeus's faith was so evident that Jesus stood still. Jesus is standing still for your move of faith.

# CHAPTER 12

## When Man Cries Out to Jesus

Now they came to Jericho. As He went out of Jericho with His disciples and a great multitude, blind Bartimaeus, the son of Timaeus, sat by the road begging. And when he heard that it was Jesus of Nazareth, he began to cry out and say, "Jesus, Son of David, have mercy on me!" Then many warned him to be quiet; but he cried out all the more, "Son of David, have mercy on me!" So Jesus stood still and commanded him to be called. Then they called the blind man, saying to him, "Be of good cheer. Rise, He is calling you." And throwing aside his garment, he rose and came to Jesus. So Jesus answered and said to him, "What do you want Me to do for you?" The blind man said to Him, "Rabboni, that I may receive my sight." Then Jesus said to him,

"Go your way; your faith has made you well."
And immediately he received his sight and
followed Jesus on the road.

Mark 10:46–52

There comes a time in our lives when we hit a brick wall—a
point of not knowing which way to go in life because none
of your options have worked and you need direction for your
life, a point when we come to realize that we don't know
which way to turn. It is at this moment we need to seek
God's direction for our lives. Hitting a brick wall can be one
of the best things that happen to us, if we make a decision
to seek God.

Too many times we think we know the answer, or
someone else does, and we make bad choices by seeking a
friend who is not doing any better than we are. I have learned
to seek people who seek God. It is at this brick wall moment
in our lives that we need to cry out to God.

You must understand that God created you for a purpose,
and it is in seeking God that we find our purpose in life.
Genesis 2:4–5 (NKJV) says:

This is the history of the heavens and the earth
when they were created, in the day that the
LORD God made the earth and the heavens,
before any plant of the field was in the earth

and before any herb of the field had grown. For the LORD God had not caused it to rain on the earth, and there was no man to till the ground.

The word "man" in Hebrew is *aw-dawn,* the same word as Adam, meaning a human being, an individual or the species mankind. God is still looking for man, or human beings, to do His work in the land He created.

We have to fight through this world. It is hard, but God is able to bring us through any difficulties we face, if only we call on His name and follow in His way of doing things. Too many times we think only of ourselves. Often we look in the eyes of our children or our spouses and can see hurt and pain we have caused to those around us and to ourselves. It is time for us to call on the name of Jesus. There is no other name by which men can be saved. We cannot find direction and purpose in life in a bottle. We cannot find it in needles, we cannot find it in crack, we cannot find it in marijuana. We cannot find it in a new car, in a new house, or in social status. We cannot find purpose in stocks and bonds, gold and silver. Nor can we find purpose in a title like bishop, presiding elder, or high potentate. My purpose and your purpose must be directed from Jesus.

While we were yet sinners, Christ died for us. That alone makes me and every person worth something. No matter what name you call yourself or what others call you, no matter what you have done in life, you are worth something because Jesus died for you.

In our text, there is a man in a fix. Bartimaeus is the son of Timaeus, which in Hebrew means "unclean"—the son of the unclean. Life finds us in unclean situations, and we are all unclean compared to Jesus. Here is this blind unclean beggar sitting on the side of the road, begging every day. Too many people are sitting on the sidelines of life begging for something good to happen in their lives, day in and day out doing the same old thing and expecting a different outcome. That's the definition of insanity. Bartimaeus knew that this day was different because of the crowd he heard approaching. His keen sense of hearing told his spirit that something was different—he felt it deep down inside. There are times in your life when something deep inside you directs your decisions.

Bartimaeus heard it was Jesus of Nazareth, and he began to cry out, "Jesus, son of David, have mercy on me!" Bartimaeus did not take time to tell Jesus all about his problems. He did not tell Jesus what everyone had done to him; he did not tell Jesus how he got in the fix he was in. He did not tell Jesus what accomplishments he had made in life before he became blind. He just said, "Have mercy on me."

Bartimaeus knew that all the money he had collected would not help his condition. He knew all his friends would someday not be available. He wanted to be set free of what held his potential back. But people around him told him to keep quiet. That is the sad tragedy still today that whenever someone wants to get their life straightened out, sometimes those around them discourages them. These people reprimanded Bartimaeus and tried to get him to be quiet, but he cried out even more and loudly, "Jesus, son of David, have mercy on me!"

**1. You must recognize your own self-worth.** Never wait for others to identify who you are. No matter what others think or say about you, you must make a decision about who you are and whose you are. Do not let others identify or define who you are. "Now they came to Jericho. As He went out of Jericho with His disciples and a great multitude, blind Bartimaeus, the son of Timaeus, sat by the road begging" (Mk. 10:46). They called him Bartimaeus, which means son of Timaeus, but we do not know his real name. It is not what you are called—it is what you answer to. You must know who you are in Christ Jesus. This world will label you, but in Jesus you are more than a conqueror through Him that loved us.

**2. You must get tired of your condition.** When you know something belongs to you, go for it. "And when he heard that it was Jesus of Nazareth, he began to cry out and say, 'Jesus, Son of David, have mercy on me!' Then many warned him to be quiet; but he cried out all the more, 'Son of David, have mercy on me!'" (Mk. 10:47–48). The Bible does not say, but I think Bartimaeus began to talk to himself when these people tried to hold him back. He got tired of his condition. Bartimaeus had the attitude that what Jesus had done for others, He would do it for him, because it is clear in calling Him the Son of David he had heard of Jesus. He must have known that Jesus spit on the ground and a blind man became seeing, that Jesus walked on water to see about His disciples, that Jesus had fed five thousand men and healed ten lepers and turned water into wine.

You must know that Jesus is God, and you must call on His name: "Now it's my time; I got to get mine. Jesus, you put the stars in the sky; the moon, the sun, and the earth belong to you; I know you can take care of my little problem." Jesus will stand still and heed your call if you call on Him. If you are sick and tired of being sick and tired, call on Jesus.

**3. You must start taking off and start putting on.** Bartimaeus took off his garment. Beggars wore clothing that identified their problem, and this garment identified Bartimaeus as being blind.

> And throwing aside his garment, he rose and came to Jesus. So Jesus answered and said to him, "What do you want Me to do for you?" The blind man said to Him, "Rabboni, that I

may receive my sight." Then Jesus said to him, "Go your way; your faith has made you well." And immediately he received his sight and followed Jesus on the road." (Mk. 10:50–52)

We must be willing to uncover ourselves when coming to Jesus; He already knows everything about you. Religion causes people to be covered. Too many Christians come to church covered and masked. They don't want anyone to see who they really are. They put on their religion on Sunday, and take it off after church. But when you have a relationship with Jesus and not with religion, you can be yourself all the time—you realize how much He loves you, and you are developing an intimate relationship with Him.

We have no righteousness of our own. Jesus imputes righteousness to us, but we must be willing to take off and put on the new. Second Corinthians 5:17 (NKJV) says, "Therefore, if anyone is in Christ, he is a new creation; old things have passed away; behold, all things have become new." Bartimaeus came to the side of the road the same old way but left new.

I don't know about you, but for me there is something about that name. Jesus will pick you up and turn you around and put your feet on solid ground. People will look at you and wonder whether it is you or not. Jesus spit on the ground and made a blind man see; his neighbors saw him and wondered whether it was him or not. They said that it looked like him but he did not walk like him. When the blind man walked, he could not see where he was going, but when Jesus makes us see, we begin to walk right, to see right, and to look right. People who thought they knew us don't know us anymore. People who ran with us don't want to run with us anymore.

It is time to take off and put on. Take off the old, and put on the new. Take off the old name tag and put on the new name that Jesus has given you. Take off the past and put on your future in Christ Jesus. Take off "I can't" and put on "I can do all things through Christ who strengthens me" (Phil. 4:13 NKJV).

"Be of good cheer arise, He is calling you"(Mk. 10:49 NKJV). When you cry out to Jesus, He will answer you, and your life will never be the same. Jesus, oh Jesus, how I love calling your name!

# CHAPTER 13

## Are You Like Bartimaeus?

Now they came to Jericho. As He went out of Jericho with His disciples and a great multitude, blind Bartimaeus, the son of Timaeus, sat by the road begging. And when he heard that it was Jesus of Nazareth, he began to cry out and say, "Jesus, Son of David, have mercy on me!" Then many warned him to be quiet; but he cried out all the more, "Son of David, have mercy on me!" So Jesus stood still and commanded him to be called. Then they called the blind man, saying to him, "Be of good cheer. Rise, He is calling you." And throwing aside his garment, he rose and came to Jesus. So Jesus answered and said to him, "What do you want Me to do for you?" The blind man said to Him, "Rabboni, that I may receive my sight." Then Jesus said to him,

"Go your way; your faith has made you well."
And immediately he received his sight and
followed Jesus on the road.

Mark 10:46–52

So many times in our daily lives, we make decisions and pass
judgment on others we come in contact with. We see people
on the side of the road with signs asking for donations. Some
signs state their condition. We all can pass judgment on those
we see begging, but what if it were you needing assistance?
Sometimes while walking we see people litter and never
stop to pick up their trash. As we drive our daily routes, we
see drivers who are distracted by their cell phone or putting
on makeup, dealing with kids, or passengers in the car and
sometimes not paying attention that the traffic light that has
change. While shopping, we notice people being rude and
disorderly to others in the store. At the restaurant, we notice
how the servers and staff are treated rudely by the patrons,
yet we never remember when we ourselves did the some of
the same actions we see others do. Most of the time we forget
our bad days and our bad treatment of others, while we stand
in judgment of those we see doing bad things to others.

I am learning that what I observe in others, I should
look within myself to see and try to address these same
faults in me, knowing I do some of the same actions I see in

others, and work to remove these faults from my own life. If I see others being upset in traffic, while shopping, or at a restaurant, I should try to see that in myself and deal with it. It may not be as extreme as what I see in others, but if it is there in me, I need to deal with it. We all need to look within ourselves to see what we see in others.

So today I ask you the question, *Are you like Bartimaeus?*

In our text, we see a blind man begging on the side of the road outside the city of Jericho. Jericho was the first city the Israelites came to once they entered the Promised Land. But in the New Testament, we find no interaction in Jericho other than Jesus coming through on His last visit to Jerusalem and in the parable Jesus tells of the man who fell by the wayside and was cared for by the Good Samaritan. As we focus on this text in Mark, we see nothing happening in Jericho except this interaction with a blind man named Bartimaeus. As we look at this begging blind man, his circumstances and his situation, the question for all of us is, *Are you like Bartimaeus?*

Your immediate response may be "No!" But please do not ignore this question. I am challenging you, as I do myself, to take a closer look at Bartimaeus, his life, his circumstance, and his situation. See whether you can find some of your traits and actions in life in Bartimaeus. You may be saying back to me, "Preacher, are you out of your mind? There is no way my life is like this poor blind man begging on the side of the road." But let us take a closer look.

**1. Bartimaeus is on the side of the road, outside the city.** Please notice that Bartimaeus is not in the city of Jericho, but outside the city: "Now they came to Jericho. As He went out of Jericho with His disciples and a great multitude, blind Bartimaeus, the son of Timaeus, sat by the road begging" (Mk. 10:46). We are never told whether he was allowed to be inside the city limits or not. We do not know if there was a city ordinance that kept beggars from being within the city limits, but we find him outside the city. It is clear that he was not in the main area of town.

How about you? Where are you sitting in your life? Are you on the side and not in the mainstream? Are you connected with the main group who makes decisions, or do you have any connections at all? Has life pushed you to the side? When decisions are made, are you part of the decision-making, or are you on the sideline? In church, are you part of the committee? Did they have a meeting and you were not informed? What about your family? Are you on the side, and your input is not valid? Is your input important, or are you overlooked because you always respond, "Whatever"? Do you respond, "I don't care what ya'll do"? Are you active in your daily life, or do you walk around with an attitude that "whatever will be, will be"? Are you sitting down at a time when you should be involved in the things around you? At work, at home, at school, at church, at social and political activities, and with your own personal relationship with Jesus, are you active? Or are you sitting on the side, outside the main activities of life? Do you live life on purpose, or just go with the flow? *Bartimaeus is on the side of the road, outside the city.* Are you like Bartimaeus, sitting on the sidelines of life and not in the main flow of things?

**2. Bartimaeus is blind and begging.** We are told about Bartimaeus's condition of being blind ("blind Bartimaeus, the son of Timaeus, sat by the road begging," Mk. 10:46b), but we are never told how he became blind. We do not know if he was born blind. Mark makes sure we understand his condition and situation in life, "blind and poor." The Greek word *blind* has a few meanings. One meaning is to be unable to see physically, and another is figurative in respect to the mind as being blind—being ignorant and slow of understanding. So blindness is both physical and mental.

There are times in our lives when others do not understand how we got in the situation we find ourselves in. They can only look at our condition and summarize within themselves how we might have got in this condition. The questions to ask ourselves are, "Am I blind to the possibilities that can change my life? Am I fumbling into darkness each and every day, missing out on the opportunities that will change my circumstances? Do I continue to blame others for where I am in life? Do I have a 'poor, poor me' attitude and want others to have pity on me? Is my condition a real reflection of who I really am? Why have my dreams not been fulfilled? Tomorrow, next week, in a year or in five years, am I still going to be blind to the possibilities and opportunities that are available? Am I still going to be 'poor' in my decision-making and thought process?"

Are you spending too much time begging God to do something in your life when He has given you power and authority in Jesus's name? *Bartimaeus is blind and begging.* Have you set up a GoFundMe page asking people to help with an unexpected expense? Whether you realize it or not, because it may not seem like begging, but you are doing the same as someone on the street corner, asking others to help you in your financial crisis. You are just not on the side of the road. So I ask you again, "Are you like Bartimaeus, blind and begging?"

**3. Bartimaeus is dressed to identify his condition.** It was a Jewish tradition and custom for those with sickness and physical conditions to identify themselves with a garment, which Bartimaeus throws aside when he rises to come to Jesus (Mk. 10:50). This move by him shows his faith in changing what identified him. The clothing let others know their condition when they were encountered, as they were instructed to stay at a distance from others, as were lepers. How about you? Are you identified by the style of clothing you wear? Do you make sure you have the latest fashions?

Mellody Hobson, who is president and co-CEO of Ariel Investments and the chairwoman of Starbucks Corporation, as quoted in *the New York Times* said, "My mother always had us dressed to the max but we could not keep our lights on." Are you dressing to impress but can't pay your bills? Is your hair styled and cut in a way that makes others take notice? How about your shoes or handbag? Are they name-brand? Is your tattoo the best ever made?

Or can you be identified by the people you hang out with and the names you can drop in a conversation? Whether you are hanging out in the sports bar drinking and socializing with Mr. Jones, Madam Eleanor, Engineer Smith, and Senator Sara Jane, or standing on the corner with a brown paper bag drinking with Tommy Lee, Willie J., Freda, and Billy Bob, what you do and how you are dressed identifies your condition.

Are you seeking something because your life is not fulfilled? If so, you are being identified by what you wear, and others know that it is you because of what you wear. *Bartimaeus is dressed to identify his condition.* Are you like Bartimaeus?

**4. Bartimaeus was sick and tired of being sick and tired.** Opportunity has come Bartimaeus's way, and he takes advantage of it:

So Jesus answered and said to him, "What do you want Me to do for you?" The blind man said to Him, "Rabboni, that I may receive my sight." Then Jesus said to him, "Go your way; your faith has made you well." And immediately he received his sight and followed Jesus on the road. (Mk. 10:51–52)

Bartimaeus could have asked for more money, better clothing, and a higher social standing in Jericho. But he knew what was holding him back: his ability to see with his own eyes, not depending on anyone else to see for him. He knew others did not have the vision for himself that he did. That is why they told him to be quiet. He did not want to keep relying on others for his survival. He may have been blind physically, but he had vison in seeing things change in his life.

How about you? What or whom are you depending on? Haven't you been blind to the possibilities and abilities within yourself for far too long? Isn't it time to throw off the old and come to Jesus completely in every area of your life? It may mean leaving others behind. It may mean cutting ties with others who want you to stay the same. It *does* mean that Jesus will give you direction and purpose in life.

Jesus is standing before you today and asking, "What do you want Me to do for you?" Are you ready to answer that question from a spiritual prospective? Anyone can ask for material things and money. You have had your Fannie Lou Hammer moment, and you are sick and tired of being sick and tired. Isn't it time for you to move into a more spiritual relationship with Jesus than you have ever had in your life before? If you have not accepted Jesus as your personal savior, now is the time. Or maybe you have already accepted Him as your personal savior. And yes, you know all the spiritual phases and songs. You know when to say 'amen' and 'praise the Lord' or when to clamp your hands together at the right time in church. Yes, you read the Bible and pray each day. And yes, you come to church regularly and attend Bible study and prayer meeting. You even tithe and give generously. Yet there is something missing in your spiritual life that nothing else satisfies.

Look at Bartimaeus again. He was ready for a change in his life, and "Jesus stood still" to hear Bartimaeus's request. Bartimaeus gave up everything that he did have and came to Jesus just as he was.

Jesus is standing still for you today. The question is, Are you ready to come to Jesus just as you are for a change in your life? *Are you like Bartimaeus?*

# CONCLUSION

Bartimaeus can teach us all a lot about life. We must never be blind to the possibilities we have within us and about us. We must always be able to see better than the world's view. Even in the midst of the storms of life, it is we, the body of Christ, the church membership, who must see the good and the possibilities present in these times of trouble. We must have a faith that works when we do not see through any situation we are in. We have been empowered by a spiritual vision that allows us to see Jesus in the midst of the storm. We must let the world know that Jesus can change any situation that arises in our lives.

Bartimaeus knew he could not go in the temple at Jerusalem, because of his condition that left him on the side of the road. Our work as the church must be to get those who are blind to the possibilities of Christ to be a part of Jesus's work. It is important for the work of the church to minister to the needs of people and empower people to minister back into the areas that Jesus found them in. I have always been excited to see a person who was a drug addict minister to drug addicts. They speak the language that they all understand each other. Can you envision Bartimaeus ministering to other blind people? We in the body of Christ, the church, must always be willing to include others and to give and accept support from those who are outside our immediate circle of friends and acquaintances.

Many times people are connected to a name or nickname, but when each of us comes to Jesus, He changes our name, He changes our outlook on life, and He changes our purpose in life. We are separated from our yesterdays and sometimes become the first in our family to be a witness for Jesus. This changes our attitude and outlook and gives us a vision. We begin to see things like never before as we come to Jesus just as we are and let Him do the changing in our lives.

This new relationship we develop with Jesus creates a thirst and hunger for righteousness never before experienced in our lives. We no longer sit on the sidelines of life but are called by Jesus to come follow Him on the road to Jerusalem as we go higher to the place of God. Our new relationship with Jesus may cause us to leave things behind and to give up relationships and habits. But the rewards ahead are better than what is left behind. This new relationship develops to a point that Jesus can ask us the question He asked Bartimaeus: "What do you want Me to do for you?" Your answer has developed to the point that your response is

Kingdom-driven. It is in this new relationship that your worship of the Lord Jesus and doing His work through your hands develops into "workship."

All these things are happening to you because you moved by faith, and your move of faith has rewarded you. When you cried out to Jesus in your time of need, you never realized where your relationship with Jesus would take you. But by faith you stood on His promises. Now you can relate to Bartimaeus and answer the question "Are you like Bartimaeus?"

Yes, I think we all can relate to Bartimaeus in one fashion or form. And yes, we want to follow Jesus into the presence of God.

May God bless you.

CPSIA information can be obtained
at www.ICGtesting.com
Printed in the USA
JSHW022145180322
24033JS00001B/47